Hall-Dare & Harvey
Of County Wexford

By

Arthur J. Kavanagh

Revised Edition 2015

Hall-Dare & Harvey of County Wexford

Copyright © Arthur J. Kavanagh 2015

Special Edition

Original illustrations/ Photographs

Hall-Dare & Harvey of County Wexford

Kavanagh, Arthur J.

Hall-Dare

The Hall-Dare connection with the world of international music began when Robert Westley Hall-Dare (3rd) invited Count John McCormick, the renowned tenor to fish the Slaney at Newtownbarry, (as it was then). The great man came for the fishing for several seasons. We can be sure he caught salmon in what was one of the best Salmon rivers in Europe, but the local ghillies said he never even hummed a tune while on the banks!

The reason the Slaney was one of the best Salmon rivers in Europe was because Mr. Hall-Dare had the foresight and vision to start a salmon hatchery on the Clody river. He sought the best advice available at the time and succeeded in improving the stocks of salmon to a remarkable degree. The river later became quite famous for the abundance of salmon that frequented its waters.

Still in a musical vein, in the middle decades of this century, Viola Tunnard an aunt of Clody Norton (nee Hall-Dare) of Newtownbarry House, an accomplished musician, was co-musical director of the English Opera Group with Sir Benjamin Brittain. She was responsible for producing many of the famous Operas at Aldburgh for the famous Aldburgh Festival.

Clody's great grandfather also had artistic flair and was a reputable water colourist. He was the adventurer in the family and travelled extensively abroad. He was educated at Eton and Oxford and when his formal education was complete he undertook the 'grand tour' as gentlemen of the time were wont to do. He was a careful diarist and kept detailed and immensely interesting accounts of his life and times.

Mrs. Norton (Clody) N.D.D., inherited the artistic genes and spent five years studying in the Byam Shaw School of Art. She then taught in the City & Guilds, in London, as Assistant to Bernard Dunstan R.A.

The Norton's main interest nowadays is their commercial Stud Farm, which has produced a myriad of winners on the flat. Among those Mrs. Norton remembers in particular are *Scottish*

Reel (Locking Stakes), *Yawa* (Grand Prix de Paris), *Lady Bentley* (Italian Oaks) and *Love You Millions* which won the Tattersall's Breeders Stakes in the Curragh in 1994. This horse was sold at Fairyhouse for a little over £10,000 in 1993 and has won ten times that for its new owner, Killybegs trawlerman Michael Doyle.

Playing Polo in the Bridge Meadow beside the Slaney before 1900

Mrs Norton's father Robert Westley, (Bobby), bred horses as a hobby and among his great winners were *Dumpty Humpty* which set up the World Speed Record in Golden Gates, Los Angeles (which stood for a number of years) and *Nor* which was 4th in the Irish Derby and later went on to win the San Louis Rey Handicap (Grade I) in America.. He also bred the dam of *Bunclody Tiger*, which he gave as a gift to local businessman and horse breeder, Andy Redmond. The *Tiger* went on to win the Galway Plate.

The Hall-Dare connection with the Newtownbarry area began in 1861, when Samuel Ashton sold the estates to Robert Westley Hall-Dare. The lands had been conveyed to Ashton in 1854 by the Encumbered Estates Court. Prior to that they had been in the possession of the Farnham/Maxwell family.

The Hall-Dares are descended from Robert Westley Hall Esq., of Wyefield and Cranbrook, High Sheriff of Essex 1821 and

M.P. for South Essex. He married Elizabeth Grafton Grafton-Dare of Romford and by royal sign manual he took the surname and arms of Dare in addition to those of Hall. Robert Westley was the grandson of Rev. Westley Hall whose maternal grandfather was Sir Robert Westley, Lord Mayor of London[1]. Interestingly Rev. Westley Hall was married to a sister of John Wesley the preacher as his first wife. She bore him thirteen children who all died in infancy. He married Robert Westley's grandmother as his second wife.

Robert Westley Hall-Dare and Elizabeth (Grafton) his wife had nine children – five sons and four daughters. They were:

Robert Westley (who bought Newtownbarry)
John Grafton (died in infancy)
Henry (see below)
Francis Marmeduke (d. unmarried in 1897)
Arthur Charles (died in infancy)
Mary Elizabeth (d. 1908 unm.)
Emma Burton (m. Thomas H. Bothamley. Died 1877.)
Anne Mildmay (died in infancy)
Elizabeth (m. Rev. J. Fussell). She died in 1882

Henry Hall-Dare was twice married. His first wife was Agatha Kekewich whose father Samuel as an M.P., D.L. and J.P. in Devon. They had two children – Blanche[2] who died in 1934 and Henry Arthur who became a Barrister (died unmarried in 1878). Henry Hall-Dare's second wife was Alice Tupper.

---

[1] Sir Robert Westley was the Sheriff of London in 1734 and Lord Mayor in 1744 - *The ancient remains, antiquities, and recent improvements of the city of London* By Henry Thomas (antiquarian.)

[2] Blanche was married to John Lee Warner and they had two children Harry Granville and Anne Agatha. Harry became a Lt. Col. in the Army. He fought in WW1 and was wounded five times. He was awarded the Military Cross for bravery in 1916 and was later awarded a D.S.O. He married his cousin Audrey Hall Dare from Newtownbarry but they had no children. Anne Agatha married Sir Eustace Gurney and they had four children who survived to adulthood.

Mr. Hall-Dare paid £83,000 for the Newtownbarry lands. He bought over 5000 acres in Wexford and almost as much in Carlow. The sale also included all the houses in the town. He was married to Frances Lambert of Beauparc, Co. Meath and they had two sons, (the youngest of whom Charles died at the age of 15), and four daughters. Frances may well have been a descendant of Lewis Lambert, the grandson of the famous Colonel Patrick Lambert of Dunmain. Lewis moved to Co. Meath after his father's death in 1747.

Mr. Hall-Dare did not live long to enjoy his Newtownbarry property and he died in 1866. He is remembered in the chancel window in the Church of Ireland as is his wife who died in 1862. There is a large rosette window over the main entrance to his memory also, and across the gable of the church the words "These stones shall be as a memorial", referring to cut granite stones in the wall. The rosette window was donated to the Church by Helen Hall-Dare.

The eldest son, also Robert Westley (2nd), married Caroline Sophia Newton, 2nd daughter of Henry Newton and Elizabeth (nee Doyne) of Mount Leinster Lodge, Co. Carlow. Henry was the eldest son of Philip and Sarah Newton who completed the building of Dunleckney House. The Newtons were connected with Bagenals the noted family who gave their name to the town - Bagenalstown. Henry Newton and his wife Elizabeth redesigned Mount Leinster Lodge to the plan of Daniel Robertson the well known architect from Huntingdon, Clonegal.

Caroline Sophia Hall-Dare started a Lace Making business modelled on the Borris enterprise, in order to give the wives of the local farm workers a supplementary income. There are numerous samples of the Newtownbarry Lace in the National Museum and also in Newtownbarry House. However when Caroline Sophia died the industry petered out.

Robert Westley (2nd) was a magistrate and a politician. In November of 1872 at a meeting of the magistrates of the county, Mr. Hall-Dare proposed an address to Queen Victoria, congratulating her on the recovery of the Prince of Wales. The address was seconded by Sir James Power of Edermine.

It was this Mr. Hall-Dare who founded the famous Newtownbarry Cricket Club, which continued in existence right up to the 1920s.

The first Hunting Pack of hounds used by the Hall-Dares was bought by his son Robert Westley (3rd). He hunted with the Island, Wexford and Carlow Hunts. The hunting tradition was kept up by his son "Bobby" who hunted the Island and Bree hunts.

The Hall-Dare residence on the site of Woodfield, which was built by the Maxwells was completed by 1868 It was begun by the first Mr. Hall-Dare and finished by his son. The family lived at that period at the Market Square in the house which for many years later was used as a Barracks.

Newtownbarry House, was the work of the eminent Northern Ireland architect Sir Charles Lanyon. Built in the Classical style, of rough ashlar (granite), the windows have surrounds of smooth ashlar with blocking. It is a two storey residence with two bays projecting at one end with a balustraded open porch. It has a most impressive staircase.

Mr. Hall-Dare's four daughters were: Olivia who married Rev. Richard Johnston of Kilmore, Co. Armagh, Mabel who married J. Theodore Bent, Ethel who married Beauchamp Bagenal, an officer in the British Army, of Bennekerry Co. Carlow and Frances who married Rev. Walter Hobson.

One of these ladies is the Miss Hall-Dare mentioned in Bassets Directory as being one of the best lady tennis players in Wexford.

Newtownbarry House

J. Theodore Bent (b.1855) was probably the most interesting of the Hall-Dare in-laws as he was a very well known explorer and archaeologist. He travelled widely in the Middle East, the Greek Islands and in Turkey. His huge collection of valuable artefacts are on permanent display in the British Museum.

He was best known for his work in Zimbabwe and in 1892 he published his work *The Ruined Cities of Mashonaland.* He wrote six books in all which mainly dealt with his travels in Asia and Africa. Mabel, his wife, accompanied him on his numerous journeys. He died from malaria in 1897.

Mrs Bent, who had contributed by her skill as a photographer and in other ways to the success of her husband's journeys, published in 1900 *Southern Arabia, Soudan* and *Sakotra,* which recorded the results of their last expedition into those regions.

Beauchamp Bagenal, Ethel's husband (they married in 1870) had an estate of over 4000 acres and was a career army officer. He was educated at Cheltenham College, Cheltenham, Gloucestershire, England and at the Royal Military College,

Sandhurst, Berkshire, England. He gained the rank of Lieutenant in the service of the 45th Regiment. He fought in the Abyssinian Campaign in 1868 and was a volunteer under Garibaldi. He succeeded to Benekerry, Carlow in 1869 following the death of his brother Walter who died at Bangalore, India. He held the office of High Sheriff of County Carlow in 1872. He was also a Deputy Lieutenant (D.L.) and Justice of the Peace (J.P.). His descendant James William Beauchamp Blackett, now resident in Scotland, visited Bunclody in 1993.

Robert Westley (2nd) died in Rome, from typhoid fever, in 1876. He had been an unsuccessful candidate in the parliamentary elections of 1868 and 1872. He was High Sheriff for Wexford. Interestingly, Mrs. Norton says that there is a tradition in the family that if the eldest son is not called Robert Westley he will die young!

Robert Westley had three sons[3] and three daughters. His eldest son was called Robert Westley (3rd) and his younger son Arthur Mildmay. His three daughters all got married, Elizabeth to John Olphert Adair (d.1926)who lived at Ballinapark, Hilda Mary to James Erskine Booth and Evelyn to Richard Bankes Barrow of Roxbury, Chertsey.

The Booths were of the same family as the Childers and the late President Erskine Childers was a cousin of Miss Evelyn Booth and her brothers Brigadier Booth and Lt. Col. Arthur Boogh. Mr. Childers often came to visit the Booths in Bunclody.

Mrs. Norton relates an intriguing story about Miss Booth. When Miss Booth was ill prior to her death, Jim and Clody used to take her out driving. On one of the trips it was agreed that they would go to a Chinese Restaurant. When Miss Booth was informed she remarked that although she was most familiar with Indian food, she had never eaten Chinese. They then began talking about India. "Of course," said Miss Booth, "Gandhi came round to visit most days!" Mrs. Norton hadn't been aware of the Gandhi connection and asked what he was like. "An Irish lawyer", was the reply.

---

[3] The eldest son John Marmeduke died in infancy.

Apparently the Brigadier was a very high official in the British Service in India. Miss Booth often visited her brother out there, and it was during her holidays that Gandhi used to drop in!

Brigadier John R. Booth was born in 1901 and was educated in England at Sandhurst military school. He fought in WW2 and received a D.S.O. His wife was Sheila Barron but they had no family. He lived in Rainsfort Lodge near Bunclody and died in 1971. The Brigadier's elder brother, Lt. Col. Arthur Booth died in 1954.

Arthur Mildmay Hall-Dare was educated at Eton and lived mainly in Ireland (Thomastown, Co. Kilkenny). He married Edith Fitzherbert and they had one son Derrick and two daughters Irene and Ena. Irene married Col. Harold Parsons[4] and Ena married Brigadier Kenneth Treseder.

Robert Westley (3rd), who was only 9 at the time of his father's death in 1876, lived until 1939. During his minority the estates were managed by a man called FitzHerbert. The land acts, giving the tenants the right to purchase their holdings, with the landlord's consent, were brought into force in the latter years of the 19th century and the early years of the 20th. Mr. Hall-Dare encouraged his tenants to buy out their holdings and the estate was reduced to its present size, about 600 acres.

Despite the reduction in land area the Hall-Dare family continued to give considerable employment to a large number of people who worked in various capacities on the estate. The saw mills operated until the late 1950s and the beautiful gardens were kept until the same time. Sadly the second World War took its toll and many of the estate operations were viable no more. Mrs. Norton remembers up to 30 people sitting down to dinner in the kitchen in the early 1940s.

---

[4] The Parsons had two sons Dr. Desmond Parsons and Major Anthony Parsons. Dr. Desmond has a son Dermot and a daughter Lucy. Major Anthony (M.C.) was later an ambassador to Iran in 1974. He had two sons Rupert and Simon and one daughter Emma.

During the time of 'the troubles', when many mansions were burnt by the I.R.A., Newtownbarry House was left untouched, because of the esteem in which the Hall-Dare family was held and because of the employment given to the locals. Another story has it that the Hall-Dares were just plain lucky. The burning party could not make up their minds whether to burn Newtownbarry House or Ballyrankin House, so a half crown was produced and a toss was called for. Newtownbarry won the toss and Ballyrankin was burned to the ground.

Robert Westley (3rd) married Helemi Gordon and they had two sons Robert Westley and Charles Grafton and two daughters Audrey[5] and Daphne (who died unmarried).

The late Robert Westly (Bobby) Hall-Dare and his wife
on their wedding day.

---

[5] Audrey married her second cousin Lt. Col. Harry Granville Lee Warner in 1917 and in 1942 she married George Eaton. She died in 1962 aged 65. She had no children.

Robert Westley's two sons , Robert and Charles were known affectionately as "Bobby" and "Charlie", and the late Daphne was a noted sportswoman. Bobby died in 1972 and his brother Charlie in 1994. The estate passed to Bobby's only daughter, Clody who married James Norton (now sadly deceased). Clody has one son, Robert, and two daughters, Alice and Lucy.

Newtownbarry House has been totally renovated in recent times and is open to the public. The beautiful gardens are now in pristine condition once more and attract huge numbers of discerning visitors.

Harvey of Kyle

"Be honest and religious, for I never saw the righteous forsaken, or their seed begging their bread." This was the advice of the man who might be considered to be the father of all Harveys, to his son. Those were the dying words of Rev. William Harvey in 1765 to Christopher the ancestor of the Kyle Harveys. Christopher repeated those very same words in his will.

The Harveys of Kyle like the Harveys of Bargy and Killiane descended from Ambrose Harvey, who according to Burke was styled "the elder of the Bridge of Bargy" (the name of the townland on which the castle of that name was built) and John Harvey of Killiane, who was a Member of Parliament in 1695. Both of these men descended from Francis Harvey who was a Sovereign (Mayor) of Wexford in 1659 and M.P. for Clonmines in 1661.

Ambrose, had one son, also called Ambrose, who, in 1677 married Susanna Cambay, of Huguenot descent, and they had one son Willam who became a parson. The Reverend William (the son of Ambrose the Younger of Bargy) who was twice married , was Rector of Mulrancan, Prebendary of Edermine and Mayor of Wexford in 1753. He had three sons, by his first marriage, and one son Christopher by his second wife. By his first marriage to Susanna Harvey he became the ancestor of the Bargy and Killiane Harveys and by his second marriage the ancestor of the Kyle Harveys.

His second marriage to Dorothea Chamney (daughter of Christopher Chamney) of Kyle, Co. Wexford, in 1740 was solemnised by the signing of a forty page marriage settlement document, by which 'Williain acquired one third of the Chamney lands in Kyle. He later managed to collect the other two thirds. They had three sons and four daughters, Rachel. Dorothea, Esther, and Ann who married respectively Rev. Hastings, John Archer, a Jamaica merchant, Benjamin Fisher of

Carlow, and Captain William Heatly. None of the women had any families except Dorothea and John Archer. Both of the younger sons married but William had no children and while James had, his own children had none and those branches died out.

Christopher, the eldest son of the second marriage of the Rev. William Harvey, to Dorothea became an eminent churchman, Rector of Kyle, Incumbent of Rathdowney, and of Rosscarbery, and Prebendary of Edermine. He was an ardent admirer of George Ogle and the Independent Volunteers and erected a pillar in Kyle to their memory in 1786. He married Rachel Nickson of Munny House, Co Wicklow. They had one son William and two daughters Dorothea and Rachel. Dorothea, married Percy Freke of Percy Lodge, later known as Tykillen. Two of Dorothea's sons succeeded to the title and vast estates of Lord Carbery of Cork, as their uncle, the then Lord Carbery, died childless. Rachel married Captain Randall.

Rev. Christopher died in 1796 and in his will, to which his nephew Beauchamp Bagenal Harvey was a witness, he made substantial provision for his then unmarried daughters and wrote this message *"As I have made them mistresses of their own fortunes, in the momentous affair of marriage, on which their happiness depends, I most earnestly entreat them that they will be cautious and prudent and take the advice of their mother."* He also entreated his son William to follow his profession or some other employment, *"so that his vacant hours will not sit too heavy on him like too many in the world, and as Providence has blessed him with good abilities, if he will exert them by perseverance he will overcome every difficulty."*

William Harvey of Kyle, who was educated in Trinity and who was called to the Irish Bar in 1792, and who lived between 1767 and 1853 married Dora Crosbie, the daughter of the Dean of Limerick, the Rev. Hon. Maurice Crosbie. They had five sons, Christopher George, James William, Maurice Crosbie, Percy Lorenzo and Henry Robert.

William was a well known liberal and one of the club of forty five, which campaigned for the franchise for Catholics and for the repeal of the Penal Laws. He was also a freeman of Wexford and with Beauchamp Bagenal his cousin and others, he was involved with the City of Wexford Association of the Friends of Constitutional Liberty and Peace. He was one of the gentlemen of the county who started up a relief committee in the winter of 1827, when there must have been a partial famine.

William Harvey was very highly thought of in the county as this extract from his obituary shows: *"At the patriarchal age of 88 William Harvey Esq., the accomplished and erudite scholar, the consistent, firm and undaunted patriot, the incorruptible but merciful magistrate, the kind and indulgent landlord, is no more. His memory will never die, so long as there is a heart in Ireland capable of feeling gratitude for the most distinguished services in the cause of civil and religious liberty, when it was unfashionable and unsafe to advocate the claims of the Irish Catholic. William Harvey, nearly seventy years back, with the zeal and fervour of youth boldly took his stand in the ranks of the oppressed and persecuted and having passed through many a trying and fiery ordeal, the mature judgement of his riper years only confirmed the early aspirations of his soul and he lived a quarter of a century after the darling object of his life had been accomplished - the charter of Catholic Emancipation."*

Christopher George the eldest son died in 1848 unmarried. During his tenure of office as the owner of Kyle he had established the Kyle Model Gardens, which covered some

11 acres and he employed a superintendent gardener to give instruction in the growing of flowers and vegetables and in bee keeping. He also built some cottage residences including Broomley House the home of the present Harveys. His attempts to improve the district included building two Swiss type cottages as schools. In addition he gave land to the Church to build a house of prayer but was opposed to giving land for a graveyard.

At this time the estate comprised some 700 acres of land in Kyle and in 1829 Christopher George also inherited the north Wexford lands of Beauchamp Bagenal Harvey which had reverted to Beauchamp's brother James after 1798. These lands comprised some 1000 acres in Ryland, Raheen, Mangan, Mandoran and in Glascarrig near the coast. The estate in the Ryland area was managed by John Murphy who had married Sophie Pine Harvey, Christopher George's niece.

Politically Christopher George was very active and campaigned for the abolition of the tithes. He was Mayor of Wexford in 1832 and the following year he refused to pay his tithes and was sent to Gaol and according to the family historians Robert and Avril Harvey, he was marched out of the Court of Conscience in his robes. After this symbolic rebellion he paid his own and a fellow prisoner's tithes on the following day and was released. In the succeeding years he was a strong supporter of the Liberator, Daniel O'Connell.

Maurice Crosbie the 3rd son was shot accidentally by an excise man in 1830. He was the co-owner with Nicholas Devereux of a Distillery at Bishopswater. Apparently the three men had been standing talking at the gate of the Distillery when a bird flew overhead. The excise man raised his gun to fire at it, but it discharged prematurely and Maurice was shot dead. The distillery which had been built in 1826, and which took a year to build, gave considerable employment in the area, and quite a number were employed making the whiskey when it went into production.

The second eldest son James William born in 1798 was disinherited, probably because of his extravagant lifestyle. However his son Crosbie William became the heir and successor to Kyle. Of all the Harveys perhaps Crosbie William was the most colourful character.

He joined the Army at the age of fifteen years as an ensign in the Coldstream Guards. Before he attained the age of seventeen he had experienced one of the most dreadful battles of the Napoleonic Wars. This was the acclaimed but dreadfully traumatic siege of the Farm of Hougomont, so critical in the battle of Waterloo. The siege lasted for many hours with most of the farm being burnt around the defending Guards. Casualties on both sides were horrendous. In the face of heavy enemy fire he was one of the men who was involved in the Closing of the Gate, for which he was afterwards decorated with the Waterloo Medal of Bravery. The Medal in now in the possession of Robert and Avril Harvey. He also saw service in India and was commissioned in the Cape Corps Infantry. He resigned from the Army in 1829.

The Waterloo Medal presented to Crosbie William Harvey.

Before dealing with the descendants of James William, it will be now convenient to look at the family ties of the remaining two men, Percy Lorenzo and Henry Robert. It was Henry Robert who was the beneficiary of Maurice who had been shot accidentally, but he disposed of his interest in the distillery in 1836. He was Mayor of Wexford in 1837. He married Eugenia Rochard, a French lady and had four sons and three daughters. The three girls were Dorothea, Francis and Isabella. They married respectively (and respectably), Edwin Lloyd, (they had four children and lived in Toulouse), Francis Pollock of Cork, (they had six children and they went to live in Toulouse), and Frank Courbis de Vicosi of Toulouse (they had four children). The descendants of these girls are still in France and are in contact with the Harveys of Broomley.

The four sons were Major William Crosbie Harvey, James Henry, Cavendish Gort and Robert Charles. Major William, who fought in the Crimea, was married but had no family. James Henry who died in 1909 married Jane Horton and they had a family in Australia. He died in Toulouse. Cavendish Gort married Emily Hungerford and had one son. Cavendish was in the Royal Navy and the Harveys think he died at sea. Nothing is known of his son. Robert Charles was in the Royal Marines and was alive in 1878, but nothing further is known of him.

Percy Lorenzo Harvey, of Kyle, b. 1801, sold his estates to his nephew, Crosbie. The descendants of Percy Lorenzo, who was married twice are now living mainly in Australia. He had no children by his first wife Anne Cuppiadge. Henry Lorenzo joined the Army when he was young and rose to the rank of Captain. He served mainly in India. He was retired the same year he got married (1829) on the grounds of ill health, having been wounded in Burma. He built Lonsdale, another Harvey residence in the 1830s. In 1857 he was High Sheriff of Wexford, At the age of 70 he emigrated to Australia with family.

His second wife was Arabella Leigh of Sion, Crossabeg and they had one son, and two daughters, Mary Elizabeth and Eva Dora who married respectively Arthur Kellet of Clonard and James Whitton. His son Percy Leigh Harvey who was born in 1855 married Edith Howlin Graves in Australia and they had seven children. He was Harbour Master in Melbourne for some time. Percy Leigh Harvey eventually came back to Ireland and came into possession of Kyle, which was sold to the Land Commission in 1914.

Captain Harvey known as 'Legs' because of his height - 6' 3"

James William, who it will be remembered was disinherited, the 2nd son of William Harvey, and a war hero, was the ancestor of the Kyle Harveys. He was married three times. His first wife was Francis Nunn Pounden, whom he married in 1824 and she survived only eleven years and left him with five young children, the youngest of whom, Crosbie William, was only five at the time of his mother's death. Four of the five children were girls, Dora Adelaide, Sophia Pine, Frances Mary and Julia Maria. They all married. Dora Adelaide married Edward Royce a member of the Royal Irish Constabulary, and Sophia Pine married John Murphy a J.P. of Ryland, Bunclody.[6]

---

[6] Interestingly Sophia Pine was an ancestor of the Foxton family of Clohamon, of whom the late Tom Foxton (Thomas Bagenal Harvey Foxton) was the last male member. He was well known as a fisherman of some note and was Manager of the Mount Leinster Anglers Fishermans Society.

Frances Mary married Edward S. Flood of Ballinaslaney and they had five daughters. Julia Maria married James H. Graves of Ballyconnigan, Co. Wexford and they had to emigrate to Australia due to financial difficulties at home. They had five children and one of the daughters Edith married Percy Leigh Harvey the son of Percy Lorenzo mentioned above.

James William's second wife was Eliza Harvey of Mount Pleasant, second daughter of John Harvey of Tagunnan and Mount Pleasant, who had inherited Bargy from Bagenal Harvey's brother James, but she died in 1847 without having any children and James William married yet again. His 3rd wife was Austrian, Henrietta Maria Selfurth. They had three sons. One of the boys joined the British Customs Service and went to India where he died. Another went to Australia where his descendants are still living and the descendants of the third son are living in England and the U.S.

The enigmatic James William himself died a bankrupt, in Cork in 1873 and his wife survived him, living until 1892.

It was Crosbie William, the eldest son of James William by his first marriage, who continued the line of Kyle down to the present owner Robert Harvey. Crosbie William married Elizabeth Anne Walker of Tykillen, Co. Wexford. He had three sons and three daughters. None of the girls married, but two went to South Africa and died there. The three sons were Thomas, St. George James, and the eldest son Captain Crosbie Charles. Thomas died unmarried in Canada and St. George James went there to join him.

In Canada, St. George James Harvey married Pauline Laurier the daughter of the Hon. Wilfrid Laurier, Prime Minister of Canada, and their descendants still live in Canada.

Captain Crosbie Charles was the father of Robert Thomas Crosbie the present owner of Broomley House. As a young man Captain Crosbie Charles went to India where he worked a tea plantation. There he joined Lumsden's Regiment in the Army and went to South Africa where he fought in the Boer War. After his father's death in 1901 he returned to Ireland and took over the management of the estate. He was a noted Agriculturist and was very interested in promoting the co - operative movement. He was instrumental in setting up the Bacon Factory in Wexford. He married Augustine Anne Leigh of Rosegarland in 1927 when he was 55 years old and they had two sons, Robert Thomas Crosbie and Christopher John, who died unmarried in 1967.

Robert Thomas married Avril Eleanor White and is the modern day representative of the most distinguished Harvey families of Bargy, Kyle and Killiane. An engineer by profession he worked in England, Africa and the Far East before coming back to Kyle. Robert and Avril have three married sons and three grandchildren.

Broomley House, Kyle

Index